D0503031

THE THIRD LITTLE
BOOK OF
Fred

Rupert Fawcett

HEADLINE

FRED WAS FINDING
MARRIAGE TO PENELOPE
INCREASINGLY CLAUSTROPHOBIC

THE THIRD LITTLE
BOOK OF
Fred

Since Rupert Fawcett invented Fred eleven years ago Fred has become something of a star with books and merchandise in several countries.

Fred's past life is documented in Rupert's thirteen previous books, *Fred*, *More Fred*, *The Extraordinary World of Fred*, *The Continued Adventures of Fred*, *Carry on Fred*, *At Home with Fred*, *Pure Fred* and *The One and Only Fred*, *The Best of Fred*, *The Little Book of Fred*, *The Best Bits of Fred*, *The Second Little Book of Fred* and *The Big Fat Fred Collection*.

The Third Little Book of Fred contains sixty-one new Fred illustrations depicting Fred and Penelope's eccentric life shadowed by their cat, Anthony.

First published in 2000
by HEADLINE BOOK PUBLISHING

10 9 8 7 6 5 4 3 2 1

Printed and bound in Great Britain by
Canale & C. S.p.A

HEADLINE BOOK PUBLISHING
A division of Hodder Headline
338 Euston Road
London NW1 3BH

www.headline.co.uk
www.hodderheadline.co.uk

FRED AND PENELOPE FELT THEY
HAD TO CLIMB THE STAIRCASE
SIMPLY BECAUSE IT WAS THERE

CONSIDERING HE WAS SUPPOSED TO
BE ALL-SEEING AND ALL-KNOWING
FRED WAS SURPRISED THAT GOD
NEEDED DIRECTIONS TO THE CHIP SHOP

PENELOPE AND THE GIRLS NEVER
GAVE UP IN THEIR BATTLE
AGAINST CELLULITE

WHEN IT CAME TO THEIR GARDEN
FRED AND PENELOPE
WERE PERFECTIONISTS

PENELOPE SOON REALISED THAT THE
ADVENTURE HOLIDAY WAS
WASTED ON FRED

BY THE FOURTH DAY OF THEIR
HOLIDAY FRED AND PENELOPE
COULD FEEL THEMSELVES
BEGINNING TO UNWIND

FOR HER BIRTHDAY PENELOPE
HAD ASKED FRED FOR A
PAIR OF MULES

FRED STILL YEARNED FOR HIS
OLD DAYS AT THE ZOO

FRED COULDN'T HELP FEELING
THAT HIS LIFE WAS
DISAPPOINTINGLY DULL

TO AVOID THE HASSLE OF WALKING
AROUND THE END OF THE BED
TO REACH THE BATHROOM FRED
CONSTRUCTED A SMALL BRIDGE

PENELOPE COULD NEVER RESIST A
MAN IN A NEW PAIR OF SLIPPERS

PENELOPE AND THE GIRLS HAD
JUST ABOUT GIVEN UP ON THEIR
CELLULITE WHEN THEY DISCOVERED
THE FULL-SPIN METHOD

THE DOCTOR HAD ADVISED PENELOPE
TO JUST GO ALONG WITH
FRED'S JUMBO JET FANTASY

FRED SUDDENLY REALISED THAT
PENELOPE'S ANTI-FOOTBALL
MOVEMENT MEANT BUSINESS

FRED FOUND THERE WAS NO
ESCAPE FROM CHRISTMAS

AT LAST PENELOPE FOUND
THE LOST HAIRGRIP

PENELOPE OFTEN WONDERED WHY
THEY COULDN'T SIMPLY BUY A TUMBLE
DRIER LIKE OTHER PEOPLE

'I THOUGHT I TOLD YOU TO STAY
AWAY FROM THAT TIME MACHINE,'
SIZZLED PENELOPE

FRED ONLY AGREED TO HIS MOTHER-
IN-LAW STAYING FOR CHRISTMAS
ON CERTAIN CONDITIONS

FRED KEPT A GOOD SUPPLY
OF FACIAL FEATURES

OVER THE YEARS PENELOPE
GRADUALLY BECAME ACCUSTOMED
TO FRED'S VARIOUS PECULIARITIES

FRED'S LATEST LABOUR-SAVING CREATION
WAS DESIGNED TO SWEEP THE FLOOR,
DUST THE CEILING AND WASH A
WINDOW ALL AT THE SAME TIME

PENELOPE HAD TO ADMIT THAT FRED'S
LATEST INVENTION THE 'ROBODOG'
WAS SURPRISINGLY REALISTIC

PENELOPE WAS BEGINNING
TO HAVE SECOND THOUGHTS
ABOUT THE PIERCED NAVEL

'HE'S BEEN WATCHING
CHANGING ROOMS AGAIN',
SIGHED PENELOPE

FRED WONDERED IF HE OUGHT TO
CONTACT PENELOPE'S FRIENDS AT
CHOCOHOLICS ANONYMOUS

FRED BEGAN EACH DAY WITH A
FEW MINUTES PRAYER AT HIS
SHRINE TO BARRY, THE
PATRON SAINT OF SLOTH

FRED MADE A MENTAL NOTE
NOT TO FORGET PENELOPE'S
BIRTHDAY AGAIN

FRED'S MOTHER-IN-LAW REALISED
SHE HAD BEEN A FOOL TO
ACCEPT HIS OFFER OF
A BIRTHDAY TRIP

FRED WAS BEGINNING TO REGRET
OFFERING TO GIVE PENELOPE
DRIVING LESSONS

FRED DERIVED IMMENSE PLEASURE
FROM WATCHING PENELOPE
CHANGE THE SHEETS

PIP HAD MANAGED A WHOLE WEEK
WITHOUT A CIGARETTE WITH A
LITTLE HELP FROM HIS
NICOTINE PATCHES

PENELOPE LIKED TO KEEP
FRED ON HIS TOES

THE TROUBLE WITH FRED'S COUSIN
WAS HE WAS ALL MOUTH

PENELOPE DECIDED TO CONFRONT
FRED WITH THEIR DECREASING
RATIO OF CUDDLES

PENELOPE LIKED TO PLAY
HARD TO GET

FRED LOVED TO SPEND A QUIET
SUNDAY AFTERNOON FISHING
FOR COMPLIMENTS

TWICE A DAY FRED AND PENELOPE
TOOK THEIR FOUR PET ANTS
FOR A WALK AROUND THE BLOCK

IF HIS FIRST DAY WAS ANYTHING TO
GO BY FRED'S CAREER AS A TREE
SURGEON WOULD BE SHORTLIVED

FRED COULDN'T HELP FEELING THAT
PENELOPE WAS MAKING THE KITCHEN
A LITTLE TOO HYGIENIC

FRED'S VEGETARIAN DIET WAS
TAKING SOME GETTING USED TO

FRED'S BAND, 'THE SILENTS' CONSISTED
OF JIM ON AIR GUITAR, FRED ON AIR
BASS, PIP ON AIR DRUMS AND
MR NESBIT ON AIR TRIANGLE

FRED'S FAVOURITE EVENT AT
THE HIGHLAND GAMES WAS
TOSSING THE WIFE

PENELOPE WAS DISAPPOINTED TO
SEE FRED AND HER MOTHER
FIGHTING AGAIN

PENELOPE SEEMED DISAPPOINTED
WITH HER NEW MOBILE PHONE

PENELOPE COULDN'T HELP FEELING
THAT FRED WAS OVER-REACTING
TO HER CREDIT CARD STATEMENT

FRED CHOSE TO IGNORE PENELOPE'S
SUGGESTION THAT HE GET
THE POOL FIRST

JUST FOR A CHANGE FRED AND
PENELOPE DECIDED TO TAKE A
DIFFERENT ROUTE HOME FROM TESCOS

IT WAS WHILST DIGGING HIS ALLOTMENT
THAT FRED ACCIDENTALLY UNEARTHED
THE ANCIENT REMAINS OF A TEMPLE
OF WORSHIP TO THE SUN GOD, RA

FRED COULDN'T WAIT TO PRESENT HIS
LATEST INVENTION, 'SYNCHRONISED
PADDLING' TO THE INTERNATIONAL
OLYMPIC FEDERATION

EVERYONE CONGRATULATED MRS NESBIT
ON MANAGING A WHOLE YEAR
WITHOUT A CIGARETTE